CEASELESS POETRY FOR YOU

MANJU P. B.

For my life.

Words from the heart

Whispered anonymously

Oh my love, without you

My poems are lifeless.

Contents

Acknowledgements

I would like to express my deepest gratitude to Shan P H, my friend, for supporting me and contributing to the creation of this book. Special thanks to P B Aswathy, Maheswari C S, Anagha Krishna and Pooja Ramesh for encouraging me. I would also like to thank my parents, friends and relatives.

An album of memories

Knocking at the door of my dream

The river of clouds

Made a blanket

To keep your memories alive

In my heart.

Every time you stare at me

 Feels like the rain in the dark

 Cold embraces me as your love

 Throughout the night.

Wandering in the moonlight

    In the amid stars

    Breath of our tales

    Joined in the journey

    To see your serene smile.

Can't imagine

    Loving you is to lose you

    Wishes to erase the day

    When you leave my hand

    If you go, I melt

    Into the solitude of wild

    Where I'm invisible

    To the world

    Cause, if you are not there

    I'm like an uninhabited

    For you, I may be an intruder

    To your heart

    But, for me

    You are the star in my life.

Breeze left unsaid

> In your absence
>
> My pen forbid me
>
> To explore the words
>
> Cause, you were beyond my touch
>
> Even the bliss of my eyes
>
> Sank in the ocean of shadow.

Your serene smile

    Hides in my eyes

    Like moonlight in the dark

    You are the light in my life

    The adorable secret of mine

    Keeps knocking at my heart.

For how long will you hide

The love resides in your life

Even the stars know your secret

Cause, my soul lives for you.

Oh, traveller

    who stole my smile

    You are the stars

    In the sky of my life

    If there is no smile in you

    Mine will fade too.

How can I fly away from you

    Even my soul resides where you are

    How can I remain silent from you

    Even my heart beats for you

    How can I live without you

    Even my life breathes for you.

I saw you in the moonlight

    I explored your mesmerizing eyes

    Feels like I'm amid the cloud fall

    I'm addicted to the way you look at me.

I searched for you

    In the blue ocean

    I have sent rain to there

    So they will give my message

    But you were far away

    Where nobody could find you

    Baby, come to the sky

    Meet me amid the sunshine

    We can embrace

    In the blanket of clouds.

Oh my life

    The hidden love that we share

    Chasing amid the words

    Every glance of yours

    Feels like waves of dreams

    That keeps my heart alive

    Unsaid story reveals

    The poem waited a lifetime

    For you.

Let's swim in the ocean of dreams
      Ceaseless kiss on this enamouring night
      Amidst our directionless heart
      We can hide our flame from this world
      Our love will be kept as a secret
      Neither afloat nor drowning.

I wandered for more than a million years

    My heart met with a tragedy

    It turned cold as a glacier

    Then you came

    You came into my life

    Like a wildfire

    You walked through the blizzard

    Without thinking twice.

You melted me with your warmth

    You raised me with your words

    I feel free as a bird when I'm with you

    Now, I wonder

    Whether you are real or an illusion.

We are like a puzzle that fits flawlessly

My heart always leads me to you

I Feel like I'm lost in you

You make me alive with your magical touch.

A bouquet of your kisses

    An ocean of your embrace

    My love for you will remain there

    Till the light and dark dies

    Cause, it is inscribed in the heart of the universe.

Flying without limits

In the light of thousand stars

Your mellifluous voice met mine

I can feel you from apart

Enchanting silence

The rhythm of solitary

Your ecstatic smile melted my heart

I'm burning for you

Without you

My poem has no life.

Till you stay in my life

  I will love you my heart out

  When you leave me

  I will melt away in this world

  With a great smile.

When I close my eyes

    An innocent bird came to my mind

    Flying high above the clouds

    Free as a wind wandering everywhere

    My heart played a symphony

    It was an incomplete one

    But when I taste the love of your mouth

    The music got its chords

    Sometimes hurt meet my soul

    Answers left my mind

    What's between us?

    Every vein in my body said out loud

    That you are the missing part of heart

    In my life.

The dreams we saw together
	I will never let it die
	Even if we are unable to fulfill
	Our souls will never leave each other
	Till the cosmos vanish.

Your euphonious voice

    Shares stories for me

    Those tulip-like lips of yours

    Melodiously explores me

    The most alluring eyes in the world met mine

    To melt in love.

Oh my love

    You are the poetry

    I never want to forget.

I wrote a song

    In the cold midnight

    The stars and moon witnessed

    The falling words from the rain of my heart.

The smiling clouds

    Twinkling stars

    Storytelling moon

    I see life

    Heard the breath of wind

    The melody of rain

    Everything says

    About you.

Charming hands of yours

 Tells stories to my skin

 Feather like lips of yours

 I sank into its sweetness.

When you look at me

    Feel like I'm walking in the paradise

    When you smile at me

    Feel like I'm flying at the top of the world.

When afloat in your dreams

I remember

How you came into my life

Into my world

It's a secret tale.

You are the precious soul

    That I searched for years

    You were the unsolved mystery

    In my heart.

A directionless bird

Flying nowhere

Heart like a mountain

Unclimbable

Mind like an invisible space

Secluded

But, you came

You break every boundary

That I created

You came into my life

Without a sign.

I melted for your love

    I will burn for you infinite times

    My love for you will remain

    In my every poem.

Each word I write

    Won't be there in the paper

    Cause the ink fades away

    In your absence.

I can love you

    More than anyone can

    In this universe

    When you forget that

    You will remember

    Through the poems

    That wrote for you

    With my burning heart.

Blue waves

> Shining sun
> Melodious wind
> The eternal love of your
> Soothing voice
> What else do I need
> In my life.

You gave me happiness

Light up

My little world

But

You remain a mystery

I feel sometimes

I don't know you

Your eyes hide something

Distance between us

Feels like diving

Into the ocean of silence.

Sleepless night

    Wandering mind

    Curious wind

    Staring stars

    What should I write about you?

    A thousand words came to my mind

    At the moment when I think about you.

How far I can go

    Without seeing you

    Wherever our journey takes us

    In the end

    I will be in your arms

    That's where my heart resides.

My life

    Only your warmth opens

    The door of my heart.

Your mischievous smile

Your sparkling brown eyes

Your wavy hair

Keeps calling me everywhere

To be with you

Your deep silence

Your unpredictable anger

The distance when you leave

It makes my heart leave

From my soul.

Epilogue

You are the wish

That I never want to cease

Cause, I can't take my eyes off you.